Sugar Grove Public Library
54 Snow St.
Sugar Grove, IL 60554

12-15-05

www.sugargrove.lib.il.us

Math All Around

Holiday Fractions

Jennifer Rozines Roy and Gregory Roy

 **Marshall Cavendish**
Benchmark
New York

Did you know that when we enjoy special days, we are using **fractions**?

A fraction is a part of a whole, as one slice of cake is part of a whole birthday cake. The world is full of fractions. If there were no fractions, we wouldn't be able to share things!

Let's celebrate holidays throughout the year and share some fraction fun!

Trick-or-treat! It's Halloween and your neighbors have been handing out your favorite chocolate bar. Your best friend gets the last one, but he gives you half.

The whole candy bar is broken into two **equal** pieces. Each piece can be written as $\frac{1}{2}$ or one-half. Half, or $\frac{1}{2}$, is a fraction.

And this fraction is delicious!

A month after Halloween, families gather around the Thanksgiving table to give thanks for good things.

A good thing on this table is dessert—one large pumpkin pie. But you don't eat the whole pie! There are other people who want some, too.

Grandma cuts the pie through the middle, making two pieces. Then another cut makes four pieces. Two more cuts and now we have eight— more than enough for each person.

Each piece of pie is called one-eighth, or $\frac{1}{8}$, which is a fraction.

Every night of Hanukkah has fraction action. Hanukkah is a Jewish festival in which families light candles each evening on a candleholder called a **menorah**.

There are eight candles—one for each day of the festival—and a "helper" candle used to light them.

On the first night of Hanukkah, one out of the nine candles is lit. The helper candle also stays lit, so $\frac{2}{9}$ of the candles are burning.

On the second night, two of the nine candles are lit. With the helper candle, that's $\frac{3}{9}$.

Each night, one more candle is lit until all nine burn brightly on the last night.

Ho! Ho! Ho! Santa Claus is coming to town! It's time to trim the Christmas tree.

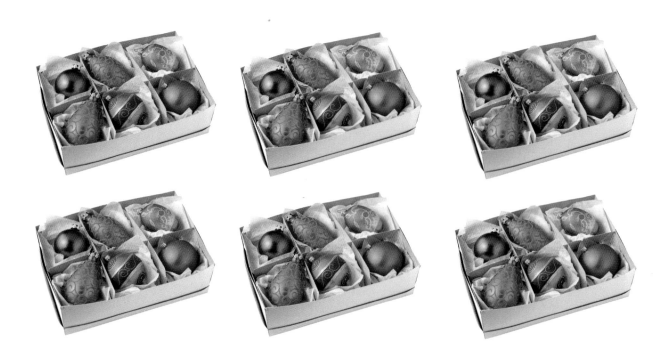

There are six boxes of Christmas balls. You get two boxes, your brother gets two boxes, and your sister gets two boxes. Each of you has two out of the six boxes. That's $\frac{2}{6}$ each.

Now everyone has an equal number of decorations. Fractions helped you to share, and they helped make the Christmas tree pretty!

Every night of Kwanzaa, you light one of the seven candles in a candleholder called the **kinara**. Each candle stands for a family value.

In the center is a black candle. What fraction of the whole set of candles is black? One out of seven, $\frac{1}{7}$ (one-seventh).

The fraction that shows how many green candles are lit is $\frac{3}{7}$ (three-sevenths), or three out of seven.

The fraction that shows how many candles are red is $\frac{3}{7}$.

When all the candles are lit, it's time to tell a story. What a wonderful way to bring the whole family together.

Every year on December 31, people around the world celebrate the arrival of a new year.

You and your family are ringing in the new year with a party at your house. You have one bag of party hats, with six hats in the bag.

What fraction tells how many party hats you'll be using? Five out of six, or $\frac{5}{6}$ (five-sixths).

A fraction has two parts—the **denominator** and the **numerator**.

The denominator is the number on the bottom of the fraction, underneath the line. It tells how many parts make up the whole. This bag has six hats, so the denominator is six.

The numerator in a fraction is the number above the line. It tells how many pieces are taken from the whole. You used five of the party hats in the bag.

numerator → 5
___
denominator → 6

In February, we make Valentine cards for our friends and family.

We fold a pile of ten pieces of red paper in half. Our first Valentine fraction is $\frac{1}{2}$. Next, we draw $\frac{1}{2}$ of a heart on the stack of paper.

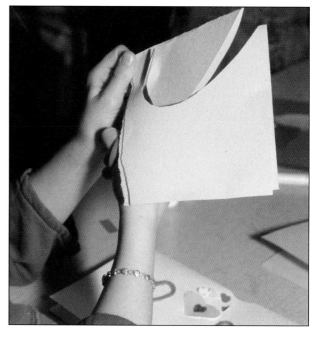

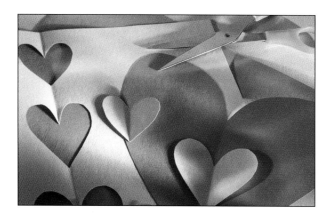

We cut on the line with scissors. When we open up the paper, we have ten whole hearts to decorate!

Let's see. You'll need one for Mom and one for Dad. That's two out of ten $\left(\frac{2}{10}\right)$ for your parents. You will need two out of ten $\left(\frac{2}{10}\right)$ for Grandma and Grandpa and five out of ten $\left(\frac{5}{10}\right)$ for your friends. And the last one out of ten $\left(\frac{1}{10}\right)$ goes to your dog. You *love* your dog!

In late spring, the United States observes Memorial Day. On Memorial Day, flags are flown to remember soldiers who died for their country.

Let's count the stripes on the flag. There are thirteen. Seven stripes are red. That fraction is $\frac{7}{13}$, seven out of thirteen.

The rest of the stripes are white. That is six out of thirteen, $\frac{6}{13}$!

What a beautiful flag to wave in honor of Memorial Day!

It's the Fourth of July! A parade marches down your street. You and two of your friends are having a picnic in the park.

While you watch the parade, your friend pulls out a tray of cupcakes from the picnic basket. *Yum!* How many will you eat?

If you ate six out of six, or $\frac{6}{6}$, that would equal one whole set of cupcakes.

$$\frac{6}{6} = 1$$

But that would make your friends mad, and your stomach would get sick!

So you choose two cupcakes—two out of six, or $\frac{2}{6}$. Each of three friends gets $\frac{2}{6}$ of the set of cupcakes. That's fair.

Take a big bite and enjoy the Fourth of July treats!

Fractions help us celebrate holidays by allowing us to be a *part* of a *whole* lot of fun!

How do you use fractions to celebrate *your* life?

Glossary

denominator—The number of a fraction that tells how many parts make up the whole.

equal—Having the same amount or number.

fraction—A part of a whole; a number that shows a part of a set.

kinara—A candleholder for seven candles used during Kwanzaa.

menorah—A candleholder for nine candles used during Hanukkah.

numerator—The number of a fraction that tells how many parts are being used.

Read More

Jones, Lynda, *Celebrate! Kids Around the World*. John Wiley & Sons, 2000.

Kindersley, Barnabas, and Anabel Kindersley, *Celebrations! Children Just Like Me*. DK Publishing, 1997.

Long, Lynette, *Fabulous Fractions*. John Wiley & Sons, 2001.

Web Sites

A+ Math
www.aplusmath.com

The Math Forum: Ask Dr. Math
http://mathforum.com/dr.math

Index

Page numbers in **boldface** are illustrations.

About the Authors

Jennifer Rozines Roy is the author of more than twenty books. A former Gifted and Talented teacher, she holds degrees in psychology and elementary education.

Gregory Roy is a civil engineer who has co-authored several books with his wife. The Roys live in upstate New York with their son Adam.

Marshall Cavendish Benchmark
99 White Plains Road
Tarrytown, New York 10591-9001
www.marshallcavendish.us

Library of Congress Cataloging-in-Publication Data

Roy, Jennifer Rozines, 1967-
Holiday fractions / by Jennifer Rozines Roy and Gregory Roy.
p. cm. — (Math all around)
Summary: "Reinforces the reader's ability to recognize and create fractions, stimulates critical thinking,
and provides students with an understanding of math in the real world"—Provided by publisher.
Includes bibliographical references and index.
ISBN 0-7614-2001-0
1. Fractions—Juvenile literature. I. Roy, Gregory. II. Title. III.Series.
QA117.R84 2005
513.2'6—dc22
2005004087

Photo Research by Anne Burns Images

Cover Photo by *Corbis*/Phillip James Corwin

The photographs in this book are used with permission and through the courtesy of:
Corbis: pp. 1, 24 Ariel Skelley; p. 4 Ed Boch; pp. 5 r, 6, 13, 19, 20 b, 21, 23, 25 (all) Royalty Free; p. 7 t Jose Luis Pelaez, Inc.;
p. 7 b Rick Barrentine; p. 17 Gary Houlder; p. 20 t Lyn Hughes; p. 27 Tom Stewart. *SuperStock*: p. 2 Ron Brown;
p. 5 l Digital Vision Ltd.; p. 8 Charles Orrico; p. 10 t b SuperStock; p. 11 Shaffer/Smith; p. 12 Brand X; pp. 14, 15 3D Studios;
p. 16 Francisco Cruz.

Series design by Virginia Pope

Printed in Malaysia
1   3   5   6   4   2